"The Freedom of Freelancing: How to Build a Successful Business on Your Own Terms"

TABLE OF CONTENTS

- "Introduction: The Benefits of Freelancing and the Path to Freedom"
- "Chapter 1: Defining Your Niche and Finding Your First Clients"
- "Chapter 2: Setting Up Your Business and Managing Finances"
- "Chapter 3: Building a Strong Online Presence and Networking"
- "Chapter 4: Time Management and Productivity for Freelancers"
- "Chapter 5: Pricing Your Services and Negotiating Contracts"
- "Chapter 6: Staying Motivated and Overcoming Impostor Syndrome"
- "Chapter 7: Growing Your Business and Scaling Up"
- "Chapter 8: Managing Risk and Planning for the Future"
- "Conclusion: Embracing the Freedom of Freelancing and Achieving Success"
- Additional Freelancing Tips
    - ☐ Networking and finding clients
    - ☐ Time management and productivity
    - ☐ Financial management and pricing strategies
    - ☐ Marketing and branding for freelancers
    - ☐ Balancing work and personal life as a freelancer

CHAPTER 1: Introduction: The Benefits of Freelancing and the Path to Freedom

Freelancing is a career path that is growing in popularity as more and more people seek greater flexibility and autonomy in their work lives. In this chapter, we will explore the many benefits of freelancing and how it can provide a path to freedom, both financially and personally.

One of the key benefits of freelancing is the flexibility it provides. As a freelancer, you have the freedom to set your own schedule and work on projects that align with your interests and skills. This can lead to a greater sense of satisfaction and fulfillment in your work.

Freelancing also provides financial benefits. As a freelancer, you have the potential to earn more money than you would as an employee, as you can charge higher rates for your services and take on multiple clients at once. Additionally, freelancing can provide a level of financial stability, as you are not dependent on a single employer for your income.

Another benefit of freelancing is the ability to work from anywhere. With the rise of remote work and digital communication tools, freelancers can easily work with clients from all over the world. This provides a level of freedom and mobility that can be hard to come by in traditional employment.

Freelancing also provides the opportunity to be your own boss. As a freelancer, you have complete control over your business and can make decisions that align with your values and goals. This autonomy can lead to greater satisfaction and a sense of pride in your work.

Freelancing also allows for the ability to continuously improve and learn new skills. By taking on a variety of projects and clients, freelancers are exposed to new industries and technologies, which can help them stay current and competitive in the job market.

Moreover, freelancing also allows for a better work-life balance. Without the rigidity of a 9-5 schedule, freelancers can create a schedule that works best for them and their families. This can lead to a better overall well-being and increased happiness.

Additionally, freelancing can also provide a sense of community. Many freelancers find support and mentorship from other freelancers, as well as from online communities and networking groups. This can be especially valuable for those just starting out on their freelancing journey.

In conclusion, freelancing can provide a path to freedom, both financially and personally. It offers a level of flexibility, autonomy, and opportunity for growth that traditional employment cannot match. The next chapters of this book will delve deeper into the different aspects of freelancing and how to build a successful and fulfilling freelance career.

Chapter 2: Setting Up Your Business and Managing Finances

Before you can start freelancing, it is important to set up your business and understand the financial aspects of running a freelance business. In this chapter, we will discuss the steps you need to take to set up your business and manage your finances effectively.

The first step in setting up your business is to choose a business structure. The most common options for freelancers are sole proprietorship, partnership, LLC, and corporation. Each structure has its own advantages and disadvantages, so it is important to research and choose the one that is best for you.

Next, you need to register your business and obtain any necessary licenses and permits. This may include registering for taxes, obtaining a business license, and registering for any industry-specific licenses. It's important to consult with a lawyer or accountant to ensure that you are in compliance with all local and state laws.

Once your business is set up, it's important to set up a separate business bank account. This will make it easier to track your expenses and income, and will also help you to maintain a clear separation between your personal and business finances.

In addition, it's important to establish a system for invoicing and collecting payment from your clients. You should decide on what billing schedule works best for you and your clients, and make sure to clearly outline your payment terms in your contracts.

Managing your finances is an essential part of running a successful freelance business. One of the most important aspects of this is keeping accurate financial records. You should keep track of all your income and expenses, and regularly review your financial statements to ensure that your business is on track.

It's also important to budget for your business. This means setting aside money for expenses such as taxes, insurance, and equipment, as well as for unexpected expenses. Having a budget will help you to stay on top of your finances and make sure that your business is financially stable.

Another important aspect of financial management is invoicing and collecting payment from your clients. It's important to invoice promptly and clearly outline your payment terms in your contracts. You should also set up a system for following up on unpaid invoices and be prepared to take legal action if necessary.

It's also important to be aware of your tax obligations as a freelancer. You will be responsible for paying your own taxes, including self-employment taxes, income taxes, and sales taxes. It's important to consult with a tax professional or use tax software to ensure that you are in compliance with all tax laws.

In addition, it's important to consider the long-term financial implications of freelancing. This includes saving for retirement, setting aside money for unexpected expenses, and planning for future financial goals.

In conclusion, setting up your business and managing your finances effectively is crucial to the success of your freelance business. By taking the time to research and understand your business structure, register your business, set up a separate bank account, and establish a system for invoicing and collecting payment, you will be well on your way to financial stability and success as a freelancer.

Chapter 3: Building a Strong Online Presence and Networking

In today's digital age, having a strong online presence is crucial for any business, including freelancing. In this chapter, we will discuss the importance of building a strong online presence and networking for freelancers, and provide tips on how to do it effectively.

The first step in building a strong online presence is to create a professional website. Your website should showcase your skills, experience, and portfolio, and should be easily navigable and visually appealing. It's also important to make sure your website is optimized for search engines, so that potential clients can easily find you.

Social media is another important aspect of building a strong online presence. Platforms such as LinkedIn, Twitter, and Facebook can be used to connect with potential clients, showcase your work, and stay current on industry news. It's important to create a consistent branding and regularly post content that showcases your skills and experience.

Creating a blog or writing articles for online publications can also help to establish you as a thought leader in your industry. By sharing your knowledge and experience, you can build trust with potential clients and establish yourself as an expert in your field.

Networking is also an important aspect of building a strong online presence. Networking events and online communities, such as LinkedIn groups, can provide opportunities to connect with potential clients, collaborators, and mentors.

Another way to network is to attend industry conferences and events. These can provide opportunities to meet potential clients and collaborators, as well as stay current on industry developments.

Also, reaching out to other freelancers and entrepreneurs in your field can be a great way to network and build relationships. By sharing your knowledge and experience, you can help each other grow your businesses and achieve success.

Online marketplaces, such as Upwork and Fiverr, can also be a great way to connect with potential clients. These platforms allow freelancers to showcase their skills and experience, and bid on projects from clients around the world.

In addition, client testimonials, recommendations, and case studies are a great way to showcase your skills and build trust with potential clients. By sharing feedback from satisfied clients, you can demonstrate the value of your services and build a strong reputation.

Moreover, creating a strong online presence and networking can also help you to stay current on industry trends and developments. By regularly reading industry publications and participating in online communities, you can stay up-to-date on the latest technologies and best practices, which can help you to stay competitive in your field.

Furthermore, building a strong online presence and networking can also help you to find and win new clients. By showcasing your skills and experience, and building relationships with potential clients and collaborators, you can increase your chances of winning new business.

In conclusion, building a strong online presence and networking are crucial for freelancers. By creating a professional website, using social media, networking, participating in industry events, and showcasing your skills and experience, you can build a strong reputation, stay current on industry trends, and find new clients. It takes time and effort, but the rewards are worth it.

Chapter 4: Time Management and Productivity for Freelancers

One of the key challenges of freelancing is managing your time and staying productive. In this chapter, we will discuss the importance of time management and productivity for freelancers, and provide tips on how to do it effectively.

The first step in managing your time and staying productive is to set clear goals for yourself. This means outlining what you want to accomplish each day, week, and month, and setting specific, measurable, and achievable targets. Having clear goals will help you to stay focused and motivated, and will also make it easier to track your progress.

Creating a schedule or to-do list can also help to manage your time and stay productive. By outlining your tasks and deadlines, and prioritizing them based on importance and urgency, you can make sure that you are focusing on the most important tasks first.

Another important aspect of time management and productivity is to minimize distractions. This means turning off your phone, closing unnecessary tabs on your computer, and finding a quiet place to work. By minimizing distractions, you can stay focused and get more done in less time.

It's also important to take regular breaks. Studies have shown that taking short breaks throughout the day can help to improve productivity and reduce burnout. This can be as simple as taking a short walk, stretching, or meditating.

In addition, setting boundaries and saying no to non-essential tasks can also help to manage your time and stay productive.

By focusing on the most important tasks and delegating or outsourcing non-essential tasks, you can free up more time to focus on the things that truly matter.

Moreover, time tracking can also be a helpful tool for freelancers. By keeping track of how much time you are spending on different tasks and projects, you can identify areas where you are wasting time and make changes accordingly.

Additionally, using productivity tools and apps can also be helpful in managing your time and staying productive. There are many apps available that can help you to stay organized, set reminders, and track your progress.

Furthermore, it's also important to set aside dedicated time for self-care and relaxation. This can help to reduce stress and burnout, and improve overall well-being.

Moreover, outsourcing or delegating some of the tasks can also be a great way to free up time and increase productivity. By outsourcing tasks such as bookkeeping, social media management, or content creation, you can free up more time to focus on the things that truly matter.

Additionally, managing your email and communication can also be a time-consuming task for freelancers. By setting aside dedicated time for email and communication, and using tools to automate or streamline the process, you can reduce the amount of time you spend on this task.

In conclusion, managing your time and staying productive are crucial for freelancers. By setting clear goals, creating a schedule or to-do list, minimizing distractions, taking regular breaks, setting boundaries and saying no to non-essential tasks, time tracking, using productivity tools and apps, outsourcing, and managing your email and communication, you can increase your productivity and achieve success as a freelancer.

Chapter 5: Pricing Your Services and Negotiating Contracts

Pricing your services and negotiating contracts are crucial aspects of freelancing. In this chapter, we will discuss the importance of pricing your services correctly and negotiating contracts effectively, and provide tips on how to do it.

The first step in pricing your services is to research the market and understand the going rates for similar services in your industry. This will give you a baseline for pricing your services and help you to be competitive.

Once you have a good understanding of market rates, you can then determine your own pricing based on your skills, experience, and costs. It's important to consider factors such as your overhead costs, taxes, and other expenses when determining your pricing.

It's also important to be transparent with your clients about your pricing. This means clearly outlining your rates, fees, and payment terms in your contracts and invoices. Being transparent about your pricing will help to build trust with your clients and reduce the likelihood of disputes.

Another important aspect of pricing your services is to be flexible. This means being willing to negotiate on price and terms, and being open to different pricing structures such as hourly rates, project rates, and retainer agreements.

Negotiating contracts is also an important aspect of freelancing. It's important to have a clear understanding of the scope of the project, the deliverables, and the timeline before entering into a contract.

It's also important to be clear about your payment terms and to include a clause that specifies when payment is due and the consequences of non-payment.

Furthermore, it's important to have a clear understanding of the rights and responsibilities of both parties before signing a contract. This includes understanding the ownership of the work, the right to use the work, and the protection of your intellectual property.

In addition, it's important to have a dispute resolution clause in your contract. This means outlining a process for resolving disputes and avoiding litigation.

Moreover, it's also important to have a termination clause in your contract. This means outlining the process for ending the contract and the consequences of termination.

Additionally, it's important to have a non-compete clause in your contract. This means that the client cannot use your work for any other projects or hire you for any other projects within a certain period of time.

In conclusion, pricing your services correctly and negotiating contracts effectively are crucial aspects of freelancing. By researching market rates, determining your own pricing, being transparent with your clients, being flexible, understanding the scope of the project, payment terms, rights and responsibilities, dispute resolution, termination, and non-compete clause, you can increase your chances of success as a freelancer.

Chapter 6: Staying Motivated and Overcoming Impostor Syndrome

Staying motivated and overcoming impostor syndrome are important challenges for freelancers. In this chapter, we will discuss the importance of staying motivated and overcoming impostor syndrome, and provide tips on how to do it effectively.

Impostor syndrome is a psychological phenomenon in which individuals doubt their accomplishments and feel like frauds. It is common among freelancers, who may feel like they are not qualified or experienced enough to be successful in their field.

To overcome impostor syndrome, it's important to understand that everyone feels this way at some point in their career. Recognizing that impostor syndrome is a common experience can help to reduce feelings of self-doubt and insecurity.

Another important aspect of overcoming impostor syndrome is to focus on your achievements and accomplishments. Keeping track of your successes and reminding yourself of your skills and experience can help to boost your confidence and reduce feelings of self-doubt.

It's also important to surround yourself with supportive people who will encourage and motivate you. Joining a community of like-minded freelancers or seeking out a mentor can provide valuable support and guidance.

Another important aspect of staying motivated is to set clear goals for yourself. This means outlining what you want to accomplish each day, week, and month, and setting specific, measurable, and achievable targets. Having clear goals will help you to stay focused and motivated, and will also make it easier to track your progress.

In addition, it's important to take care of yourself both physically and mentally. This means getting enough sleep, eating well, and engaging in regular exercise. Taking care of yourself can help to reduce stress and improve overall well-being, which can help to increase motivation.

Furthermore, it's important to set boundaries and learn to say no to non-essential tasks. By focusing on the most important tasks and delegating or outsourcing non-essential tasks, you can free up more time to focus on the things that truly matter.

Moreover, it's important to celebrate your successes and reward yourself for achievements. This can help to boost your motivation and give you something to look forward to.

Additionally, it's important to be realistic about your expectations and not put too much pressure on yourself. Understanding that progress takes time and that setbacks are a natural part of the process can help to reduce stress and increase motivation.

In conclusion, staying motivated and overcoming impostor syndrome are important challenges for freelancers. By understanding that impostor syndrome is a common experience, focusing on your achievements, surrounding yourself with supportive people, setting clear goals, taking care of yourself, setting boundaries, celebrating your successes, being realistic about your expectations and recognizing that progress takes time, you can increase your chances of success as a freelancer.

Chapter 7: Growing Your Business and Scaling Up

Growing your business and scaling up are important aspects of freelancing. In this chapter, we will discuss the importance of growing your business and scaling up, and provide tips on how to do it effectively.

The first step in growing your business is to set clear goals for growth. This means outlining what you want to achieve in terms of revenue, client base, and services offered. Having clear goals will help you to stay focused and motivated, and will also make it easier to track your progress.

Once you have clear goals in place, it's important to focus on marketing and promotion. This means identifying your target market, creating a marketing plan, and implementing strategies to reach your target audience.

Networking is also an important aspect of growing your business. This means connecting with potential clients, collaborators, and industry leaders, and building relationships that can lead to new business opportunities.

Another important aspect of growing your business is to diversify your services. This means expanding the range of services you offer to attract new clients and increase revenue.

Another aspect of growing your business is to consider hiring a team to help with the workload. This can include hiring employees, freelancers, or contractors to help with specific tasks.

Furthermore, it's important to focus on building a strong online presence. This means creating a professional website, using social media, and networking.

In addition, building a strong reputation is also important for growing your business. This can be achieved by providing excellent customer service, delivering high-quality work, and getting positive reviews and testimonials.

Moreover, it's important to stay current on industry trends and developments. This means reading industry publications, participating in online communities, and attending conferences and events.

Additionally, it's important to consider expanding to new markets or geographic locations. This can help to increase revenue and grow your client base.

In conclusion, growing your business and scaling up are important aspects of freelancing. By setting clear goals, focusing on marketing and promotion, networking, diversifying services, hiring a team, building a strong online presence, building a strong reputation, staying current on industry trends, and expanding to new markets, you can increase your chances of success as a freelancer.

Chapter 8: Managing Risk and Planning for the Future

Managing risk and planning for the future are important aspects of freelancing. In this chapter, we will discuss the importance of managing risk and planning for the future, and provide tips on how to do it effectively.

The first step in managing risk is to identify potential risks that may impact your business. This includes risks related to your industry, clients, and market conditions. Once potential risks are identified, you can then develop a plan to mitigate or manage them.

Another important aspect of managing risk is to have a contingency plan in place. This means having a plan in place to deal with unexpected events or situations that may impact your business. A contingency plan can include measures such as having extra savings or diversifying your income streams.

It's also important to have insurance in place to protect your business. This includes insurance for property, liability, and worker's compensation.

Another important aspect of managing risk is to have a clear understanding of the terms and conditions of your contracts. This means understanding the rights and responsibilities of both parties, and including dispute resolution and termination clauses.

Another important aspect of managing risk is to have a clear understanding of the legal and tax implications of your business. This means understanding the laws and regulations that apply to your business, and seeking advice from a lawyer or accountant when necessary.

Furthermore, it's important to keep accurate and complete financial records. This means keeping track of your income and expenses, and having a clear understanding of your financial situation.

In addition, it's important to plan for the future. This means setting long-term goals, creating a retirement plan, and saving for emergencies.

Moreover, it's also important to consider a plan for exiting your business. This can include selling your business, passing it on to a family member or employee, or closing it down.

Additionally, it's important to build a network of support. This can include seeking out a mentor, joining a community of like-minded freelancers, and building relationships with other entrepreneurs.

In conclusion, managing risk and planning for the future are important aspects of freelancing. By identifying potential risks, having a contingency plan, having insurance, having a clear understanding of contract terms, understanding legal and tax implications, keeping accurate financial records, planning for the future, having a plan for exiting the business, and building a network of support, you can increase your chances of success as a freelancer.

Conclusion: Embracing the Freedom of Freelancing and Achieving Success

In this book, we have discussed the many benefits of freelancing and the path to freedom that it can provide. We have also covered various aspects of freelancing such as setting up your business, managing finances, building a strong online presence, time management and productivity, pricing your services and negotiating contracts, staying motivated and overcoming impostor syndrome, growing your business and scaling up and managing risk and planning for the future.

As a freelancer, it is important to understand that there will be challenges, but with a clear strategy and an entrepreneurial mindset, success can be achieved. It is also important to remember that success is not only measured by financial gain, but also by personal growth and the ability to live a life of freedom.

It is important to remember that freelancing is not for everyone and it's not a quick fix for success. It requires hard work, dedication, and a willingness to take risks. But for those who are willing to put in the effort, the rewards can be significant.

As a freelancer, it's also important to continue learning and growing. This means staying current on industry trends, seeking out new opportunities, and building a strong network of support.

In conclusion, freelancing can be a rewarding and fulfilling career path. Embracing the freedom that it provides and having a clear strategy, an entrepreneurial mindset, willingness to take risks, hard work and dedication, continuous learning, and personal growth can help to increase your chances of success as a freelancer. Remember to celebrate your successes and learn from your failures. It's important to remember that freelancing is a journey, not a destination, and to enjoy the ride!

Networking and Finding Clients

Networking is an essential part of building a successful freelancing business. It allows you to connect with other professionals in your industry, build relationships, and ultimately find new clients. In this chapter, we will discuss the importance of networking and provide tips on how to effectively network and find clients.

The Importance of Networking
Networking is essential for freelancers because it allows you to connect with other professionals in your industry. Building relationships with other freelancers, entrepreneurs, and industry leaders can help you learn about new opportunities, stay up-to-date on industry trends, and gain valuable insights into the business.

Networking Opportunities
There are many opportunities to network, both online and offline. Online networking platforms such as LinkedIn, Twitter, and Facebook can be great places to connect with other professionals in your industry. Offline networking events such as conferences, meetups, and networking groups are also great ways to meet new people and build relationships.

Building Relationships
Networking is not just about collecting business cards, it's about building relationships. When you meet someone new, take the time to get to know them and find out what they do. Ask questions and show genuine interest in what they do. Remember, networking is about building relationships, not just collecting contacts.

Follow Up

After meeting someone new, follow up with them. Send them an email or connect with them on LinkedIn. This is a great way to keep the conversation going and continue to build the relationship.

Networking Events
Networking events such as conferences, meetups, and networking groups are great opportunities to meet new people and build relationships. Attend these events with a goal in mind, such as meeting three new people or learning about a specific topic.

Leverage Social Media
Social media is a great tool for networking. You can connect with other professionals in your industry, share your work and gain visibility. LinkedIn is a great platform for networking and finding new clients.

Attend Conferences
Attending conferences is a great way to learn about new opportunities, stay up-to-date on industry trends, and meet other professionals in your industry. Conferences are also a great opportunity to network and make new connections.

Join Professional Organizations
Joining professional organizations is a great way to connect with other professionals in your industry. Many organizations host networking events and provide opportunities for members to connect and collaborate.

Offer Help
Offering to help others is a great way to build relationships. Whether it's offering to introduce someone to a potential client

or providing valuable resources, helping others is a great way to build trust and create mutually beneficial relationships.

Be Yourself
Networking can be uncomfortable, but it's important to be yourself. Be genuine, be authentic, and don't try to be someone you're not. People can sense when you're not being genuine, and it will be harder to build relationships.

Follow Up with Leads
When you meet someone new and they express interest in your services, follow up with them. Send them an email or connect with them on LinkedIn. This is a great way to keep the conversation going and potentially turn them into a client.

Cold Outreach
Cold outreach is when you reach out to potential clients that you haven't met before. This can be done through email, LinkedIn, or even by phone. When doing cold outreach, make sure to be professional and provide value to the potential client.

Referrals
Referrals are one of the best ways to find new clients. Ask your current clients if they know of anyone who may be in need of your services, and make sure to always ask for a referral after completing a project.

Building a Strong Online Presence
Having a strong online presence is crucial for networking and finding new clients. Make sure your website, LinkedIn profile, and other online platforms are up-to-date and showcase your skills and experience.

Networking Takes Time
Networking takes time and effort, but it is an essential part of building a successful freelancing business. Make sure to set aside time each week to network, whether it's attending events, connecting with people online, or following up with leads. Remember, building relationships takes time, but it's worth it in the long run.

In conclusion, networking is a key part of building a successful freelancing business. By connecting with other professionals in your industry, building relationships, and effectively reaching out to potential clients, you can increase your chances of finding new clients and growing your business. Remember, networking takes time and effort, but it's worth it in the long run.

Time Management and Productivity

Time management and productivity are crucial for freelancers who want to build a successful business. As a freelancer, you have the freedom to create your own schedule, but it's also important to manage your time effectively to ensure that you are able to complete your work and meet deadlines. In this chapter, we will discuss the importance of time management and productivity, and provide tips on how to manage your time effectively.

The Importance of Time Management
Time management is essential for freelancers because it allows you to complete your work and meet deadlines. By managing your time effectively, you can ensure that you are able to complete your work and achieve your goals.

The Importance of Productivity
Productivity is essential for freelancers because it allows you to get more done in less time. By being productive, you can ensure that you are able to complete your work and meet deadlines, even with a busy schedule.

Setting Goals
Setting goals is an important part of time management and productivity. By setting goals, you can ensure that you are working towards something specific and that you are making progress towards achieving your goals.

Prioritizing Tasks
Prioritizing tasks is an important part of time management and productivity. By prioritizing your tasks, you can ensure that you are working on the most important tasks first, which will help you to achieve your goals.

Creating a Schedule
Creating a schedule is an important part of time management and productivity. By creating a schedule, you can ensure that you are able to complete your work and meet deadlines.

Sticking to your Schedule
Sticking to your schedule is essential for time management and productivity. By sticking to your schedule, you can ensure that you are able to complete your work and meet deadlines.

Managing Distractions
Managing distractions is an important part of time management and productivity. By managing distractions, you can ensure that you are able to focus on your work and complete your tasks.

Taking Breaks
Taking breaks is an important part of time management and productivity. By taking breaks, you can ensure that you are able to recharge and refocus, which will help you to complete your work and meet deadlines.

Using Productivity Tools
Using productivity tools is an important part of time management and productivity. By using tools such as calendars, to-do lists, and time tracking apps, you can ensure that you are able to manage your time effectively and be productive.

Eliminating Time Wasters
Eliminating time wasters is an important part of time management and productivity. By eliminating activities that

waste your time, you can ensure that you are able to complete your work and meet deadlines.

Delegating Tasks

Delegating tasks is an important part of time management and productivity. By delegating tasks, you can ensure that you are able to focus on your most important tasks and that you are able to complete your work and meet deadlines.

Staying Organized

Staying organized is an important part of time management and productivity. By staying organized, you can ensure that you are able to complete your work and meet deadlines.

Keeping a Positive Attitude

Keeping a positive attitude is an important part of time management and productivity. By keeping a positive attitude, you can ensure that you are able to complete your work and meet deadlines.

Avoiding Burnout

Avoiding burnout is an important part of time management and productivity. By avoiding burnout, you can ensure that you are able to complete your work and meet deadlines.

Financial Management and Pricing Strategies

Financial management and pricing strategies are essential for freelancers who want to build a successful business. As a freelancer, it's important to manage your finances effectively and to have a pricing strategy that allows you to charge what you're worth and maintain profitability. In this chapter, we will discuss the importance of financial management and pricing strategies and provide tips on how to manage your finances and price your services effectively.

The Importance of Financial Management
Financial management is essential for freelancers because it allows you to manage your finances effectively and to achieve your financial goals. By managing your finances effectively, you can ensure that you are able to maintain profitability and achieve financial stability.

Setting Financial Goals
Setting financial goals is an important part of financial management. By setting financial goals, you can ensure that you are working towards something specific and that you are making progress towards achieving your financial goals.

Budgeting
Budgeting is an important part of financial management. By creating a budget, you can ensure that you are able to manage your finances effectively and to achieve your financial goals.

Keeping Track of Expenses
Keeping track of expenses is an important part of financial management. By keeping track of expenses, you can ensure that you are able to manage your finances effectively and to achieve your financial goals.

The Importance of Pricing Strategies
Pricing strategies are essential for freelancers because they allow you to charge what you're worth and maintain profitability. By having a pricing strategy, you can ensure that you are able to charge what you're worth and to achieve your financial goals.

Understanding Your Costs
Understanding your costs is an important part of pricing strategies. By understanding your costs, you can ensure that you are able to price your services effectively and to achieve your financial goals.

Market Research
Market research is an important part of pricing strategies. By researching the market, you can ensure that you are aware of the going rates for similar services and able to price your services competitively.

Communicating Your Value
Communicating your value is an important part of pricing strategies. By communicating your value, you can ensure that your clients understand the value of your services and are willing to pay a fair price.

Negotiating Rates
Negotiating rates is an important part of pricing strategies. By negotiating rates, you can ensure that you are able to charge what you're worth and to achieve your financial goals.

Continuously Evaluate and Adapt
Continuously evaluate and adapt your financial management and pricing strategies. As your business grows, so will your

expenses, and the market prices may change, so it's important to continuously evaluate and adapt your strategies to ensure that you are able to maintain profitability and achieve your financial goals.

In conclusion, financial management and pricing strategies are essential for freelancers who want to build a successful business. By managing your finances effectively and having a pricing strategy that allows you to charge what you're worth and maintain profitability, you can ensure that you are able to achieve your financial goals and build a successful business. Remember, financial management and pricing strategies are not a one-time process, it's important to continuously evaluate and adapt them as your business evolves.

Marketing and Branding for Freelancers

Marketing and branding are essential for freelancers who want to build a successful business. As a freelancer, it's important to market your services effectively and to establish a strong brand that sets you apart from the competition. In this chapter, we will discuss the importance of marketing and branding and provide tips on how to market your services effectively and establish a strong brand.

The Importance of Marketing
Marketing is essential for freelancers because it allows you to reach potential clients and to build a successful business. By marketing your services effectively, you can ensure that you are able to attract new clients and grow your business.

Establishing a Brand
Establishing a brand is an important part of marketing. By establishing a strong brand, you can ensure that you are able to set yourself apart from the competition and attract new clients.

Building a Website
Building a website is an important part of marketing. By building a website, you can ensure that you are able to showcase your services and attract new clients.

Utilizing Social Media
Utilizing social media is an important part of marketing. By utilizing social media, you can ensure that you are able to reach potential clients and build a strong online presence.

Content Marketing

Content marketing is an important part of marketing. By creating valuable content, you can attract potential clients and establish yourself as an expert in your field.

Networking
Networking is an important part of marketing. By networking, you can connect with potential clients and establish relationships that can lead to new business opportunities.

Offering Free Samples or Consultations
Offering free samples or consultations is an important part of marketing. By offering free samples or consultations, you can attract potential clients and showcase the value of your services.

Referral Marketing
Referral marketing is an important part of marketing. By asking satisfied clients to refer their friends and colleagues, you can attract new clients and grow your business.

Building a Strong Email List
Building a strong email list is an important part of marketing. By building a strong email list, you can ensure that you are able to reach potential clients and keep them informed about your services.

Continuously Evaluate and Adapt
Marketing and branding strategies are not a one-time process, it's important to continuously evaluate and adapt them as your business evolves. Keep track of your marketing efforts and measure the results, so you can make informed decisions about how to improve your strategies and reach more potential clients.

In conclusion, marketing and branding are essential for freelancers who want to build a successful business. By marketing your services effectively and establishing a strong brand, you can attract new clients and build a successful business. Remember, marketing and branding strategies are not a one-time process, it's important to continuously evaluate and adapt them as your business evolves.

Balancing Work and Personal Life as a Freelancer

Balancing work and personal life is crucial for freelancers who want to build a successful business while maintaining a healthy work-life balance. As a freelancer, you have the freedom to create your own schedule, but it's also important to set boundaries and manage your time effectively to ensure that you are able to complete your work and maintain a balance between your work and personal life. In this chapter, we will discuss the importance of balancing work and personal life and provide tips on how to manage your time effectively and maintain a healthy work-life balance.

The Importance of Work-Life Balance
Work-life balance is essential for freelancers because it allows you to maintain a healthy balance between your work and personal life. By maintaining a balance between your work and personal life, you can ensure that you are able to complete your work and maintain a healthy and fulfilled life outside of work.

Setting Boundaries
Setting boundaries is an important part of balancing work and personal life. By setting boundaries, you can ensure that you are able to complete your work and maintain a balance between your work and personal life.

Creating a Schedule
Creating a schedule is an important part of balancing work and personal life. By creating a schedule, you can ensure that you are able to complete your work and maintain a balance between your work and personal life.

Prioritizing Tasks

Prioritizing tasks is an important part of balancing work and personal life. By prioritizing your tasks, you can ensure that you are able to complete your most important work while also making time for your personal life.

Managing Distractions

Managing distractions is an important part of balancing work and personal life. By managing distractions, you can ensure that you are able to focus on your work and maintain a balance between your work and personal life.

Taking Breaks

Taking breaks is an important part of balancing work and personal life. By taking breaks, you can ensure that you are able to recharge

www.ingramcontent.com/pod-product-compliance
Lightning Source LLC
Chambersburg PA
CBHW050321220526
45465CB00005B/2083